Body
SCIENCE

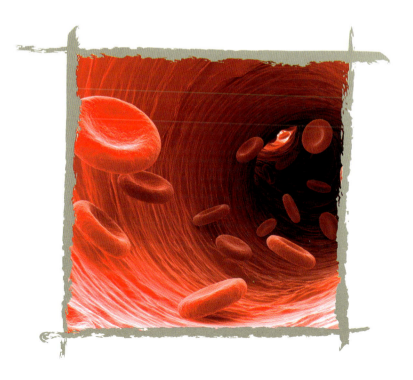

First published in 2013 by Miles Kelly Publishing Ltd, Harding's Barn, Bardfield End Green, Thaxted, Essex, CM6 3PX, UK

Copyright © Miles Kelly Publishing Ltd 2012

© 2014 Discovery Communications, LLC. Discovery Explore Your World™ and the Discovery Explore Your World™ logo are trademarks of Discovery Communications, LLC, used under license. All rights reserved. discoveryuk.com

This edition published in 2014

10 9 8 7 6 5 4 3 2 1

Publishing Director Belinda Gallagher
Creative Director Jo Cowan
Managing Editors Amanda Askew, Rosie Neave
Managing Designer Simon Lee
Proofreaders Carly Blake, Claire Philip
Production Manager Elizabeth Collins
Image Manager Liberty Newton
Reprographics Stephan Davis, Thom Allaway

All rights reserved. No part of this publication may be reproduced, stored in a retrieval system, or transmitted by any means, electronic, mechanical, photocopying, recording or otherwise, without the prior permission of the copyright holder.

ISBN 978-1-78209-527-9

Printed in China

British Library Cataloguing-in-Publication Data
A catalogue record for this book is available from the British Library

Made with paper from a sustainable forest

www.mileskelly.net
info@mileskelly.net

ACKNOWLEDGMENTS

The publishers would like to thank the following sources for the use of their photographs:

KEY t=top, b=bottom, c=center, l=left, r=right
AL=Alamy, B=Bridgeman, CO=Corbis, F=Fotolia, FLPA=Frank Lane Picture Agency, GI=Getty Images, IS=istockphoto.com, NPL=Nature Picture Library, PL=Photolibrary, RF=Rex Features, SPL=Science Photo Library, S=Shutterstock, TF=Topfoto

COVER Lightspring/S, Sebastian Kaulitzki/S **BACK COVER** F
1 Istock; **2** Pedro Nogueira/S; **3**(bg) Pixel Embargo/S, (strip, left to right) Michal Kowalski/S, Kannanimages/S, pio3/S, Andrea Danti/S, Eugen Shevchenko/S; **4–5** Segalen/Phanie /RF; **6–7** aliisik/S, Sarunyu_foto/S, aopsan/S; **6**(tr) Willdidthis/S, (tr) R-studio/S; **7** Cordelia Molloy/S/SPL, (b) Viacheslav A. Zotov/S, (bl) vvoe/S, (br) Andrea Danti/S, (tl) Twelve/S, (tl) SeDmi/S; **8** Steve Gschmeissner/SPL, (br) SPL/GI; **9** Dr. Kessel & Dr. Kardon/Tissues & Organs/GI, (bl) Alexey Khromushin/F, (br) J.C. Revy, ISM/SPL, (t) Aaron Amat/S; **10–11** Science Picture Co/GI, Palsur/S; **10**(bl) GRei/S, (bl) Linali/S; **12–13** R-studio/S, (tc) TebNad/S; **12**(bl) Michal Kowalski/S, (bl) R. Bick, B. Poindexter, Ut Medical School/SPL, (br) Litvinenko Anastasia/S, (br) Olivier Le Queinec/S, (br) B Calkins/S, (cl) kedrov/S, (cr) Nixx Photography/S, (cr) Anusorn P nachol/S, (cr) Prof. P. Motta/Dept. of Anatomy/University "La Sapienza", Rome/SPL, (tl) Oleksii Natykach/S, (tl) ZoneFatal/S, (tl) wmedien/S, (tl) ojka/S, (tr) Yevgen Kotyukh/S; **13**(bl) happykanppy/S, (br) Anthony DiChello/S, (cl) Scimat/SPL, (cr) nikkytok/S, (tl) Yaraz/S, (tl) Steve Gschmeissner/SPL, (tr) Volker Steger/SPL; **14–15** Sergey Panteleev/IS; **14**(bl) St Bartholomew's Hospital/SPL, (br) Paul Gunning/S, (cr) Fedor Kondratenko/S; **15**(br) SPL, (t) Dr. Richard Kessel & Dr. Randy Kardon/Tissues & Organs/Visuals Unlimited/CO; **16** Leigh Prather/S, (br) Diego Cervo/S, (cr) Mikhail/S, (cr) Bill Longcore/SPL, (cl) Scientifica/GI, (tr) Ozerina Anna/S; **17** Gunnar Pippel/S, (r) Colleen Petch/Newspix/RF, (bc) Alex Staroseltsev/S, (bl) AFP/GI, (bl) Alex Varlakov/IS, (br) Martin Dohrn/SPL, (cr) Alex011973/S, (tl) Eric Gevaert/S; **18–19** Neliyana Kostadinova/S, Ramon Andrade 3Dciencia/SPL; **18**(br) 3d4medical.com/SPL, (l) Sebastian Kaulitzki/S, (l) Zephyr/SPL; **19**(tr) Sovereign, ISM/SPL; **20–21** Medical Images, Universal Images Group/SPL; **20**(bl) Sergey Furtaev/S, (cr) Steve Gschmeissner/SPL; **21**(bl) Gunnar Pippel/S, (br) Kannanimages/S, (tl) Similar Images Preview/GI;

22–23 pio3/S, Eky Studio/S, Mark Beckwith/S; **22**(bl) Pascal Goetgheluck/SPL, (tr) Suren Manvelyan/RF; **23**(br) Anatomical Travelogue/SPL, (cl) Ralph C. Eagle, Jr/SPL, (cr) Omikron/SPL, (tr) guido nardacci/S; **24–25**(c) Dragana Gerasimoski/S, (tc) Carolina Biological Supply Co/Visuals Unlimited, Inc/SPL; **24**(bc) Dr Yorgos Nikas/SPL, (tl) Medi-Mation/GI; **25**(bl) Zephyr/SPL, (br) Eugen Shevchenko/S, (tr) Simon Fraser/SPL; **26**(bc) Monika Wisniewska/S, (r) Monkey Business Images/S; **27**(r) Troels Graugaard/IS, (r) Yuri Arcurs/S, (bc) Kais Tolmats/IS, (tc) 4x6/IS; **28–29** Franck Boston/S, (c) Friedrich Saurer/SPL; **28**(bl) Thomas Deerinck, NCMIR/SPL, (cl) Frederick R. Matzen/S, (tr) Aptyp_koK/S; **29**(bc) Olga Lipatova/S, (br) Professors P.M. Motta, P.M. Andrews, K.R. Porter & J. Vial/SPL, (tr) Don Fawcett/SPL; **30–31**(c) Gustoimages/GI, **30**(bc) SPL/GI, (bl) ImageryMajestic/S, (tr) Steve Gschmeissner/SPL; **31**(br) Netfalls–Remy Musser/S, (cl) Gustoimages/GI, (tc) Susumu Nishinaga/SPL; **32–33** blackred/IS, Skocko/S, Angela Harburn/S; **32**(bl) Thierry Berrod, Mona Lisa Production/SPL, (br) Power and Syred/SPL, (t) D. Kucharski & K. Kucharska/S, (t) Ultrashock/S, (tl) Retrofile/GI; **33**(bl) Francis Leroy, Biocosmos/SPL, (br) Coneyl Jay/SPL, (tr) Dr. Richard Kessel & Dr. Gene Shih, Visuals Unlimited/SPL; **34–35** Ford Photography/S, Nata-Lia/S; **34**(cl) Andrew Taylor/S, (tl) Falkiewicz Henryk/S, (tl) Igor Kovalchuk/S, (tr) Picsfive/S, (tr) Johanna Goodyear/S; **35**(tl) discpicture/S, (tl) Marilyn Volan/S; **36–37** saicle/S; **36**(l) Murdoch Ferguson/RF; **37**(bl) Mark Carrel/S, (bl) Library Of Congress/SPL, (br) Dr Yorgos Nikas/SPL, (tr) Zephyr/GI, (tr) Gordan/S, (tr) SAM OGDEN/SPL; **38–39** robertlamphoto/S; **38**(bl) kanate/S, (c) Sukharevskyy Dmytro (nevodka)/S, (cl) Dee Breger/SPL, (t) David Mack/SPL; **39**(br) Lusoimages/S, (br) Michael W. Davidson/SPL, (cl) Paul A. Souders/CO, (tr) Nils Jorgensen/RF

All other photographs are from: Corel, digitalSTOCK, digitalvision, Dreamstime.com, Fotolia.com, iStockphoto.com, John Foxx, PhotoAlto, PhotoDisc, PhotoEssentials, PhotoPro, Stockbyte

Every effort has been made to acknowledge the source and copyright holder of each picture. The publishers apologise for any unintentional errors or omissions.

Body
SCIENCE

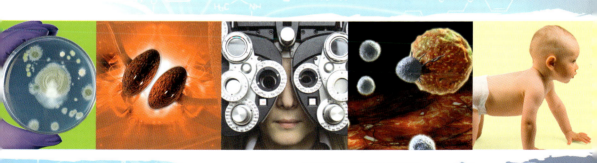

John Farndon
Consultant: Ian Graham

Miles Kelly

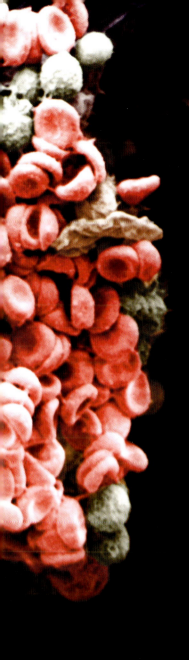

CONTENTS

Building the Body	6
Wild Landscape	8
Cellular Cosmos	10
Chemical Plant	12
Vital Juice	14
Body Heat	16
Human Computer	18
Body Signaling	20
Eye Opener	22
New Life	24
Growth Factor	26
Muscle Power	28
Strong Structure	30
Alien Invaders	32
Body Defenders!	34
Repair and Rebuild	36
Chemical Messengers	38
Index	40

◀ A scanning electron microscope (SEM) reveals a clot of red and white blood cells in a blood vessel.

Building THE BODY

The body is made up of 12 different, interlinking systems—each one performs a particular task, but they are all dependent on each other. Some, such as the circulatory system, spread throughout the body. Others, such as the digestive system, are mainly in one place.

INNARDS

1 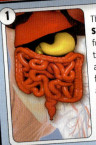 The **digestive system** breaks down food into chemicals that the body can absorb and use for fuel and materials, and then removes the rest as waste. It includes the stomach, intestines, and anus.

2 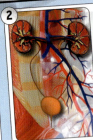 The **urinary system** removes excess water as urine. It also gets rid of impurities in the blood. It includes the kidneys and bladder.

3 The **reproductive system** consists of the sex organs that enable humans to have children. Males have a penis, scrotum, and testicles. Females have a uterus, cervix, vagina, fallopian tubes, and ovaries.

FRAMEWORK AND WEATHERPROOFING

4  The **muscular system** is made up of three types of muscle—skeletal, smooth, and heart. It circulates blood around the body and enables it to move.

5 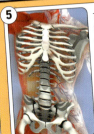 The **skeletal system** consists of bone, cartilage, and ligaments. It supports the body, protects the major organs, and also provides an anchor for the muscles.

6  The **integumentary system**—the skin—protects the body and helps to keep it at the correct temperature. The system is also the largest sense receptor, responding to touch, pressure, heat, and cold.

WIRING AND CONTROL

7 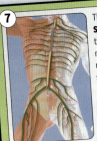 The **nervous system** contains the brain and the nerves. The brain receives electrical signals from the body via nerves and quickly sends back a response.

8  The **endocrine system** controls body processes. It releases floods of chemical messages called hormones into the blood from glands around the body.

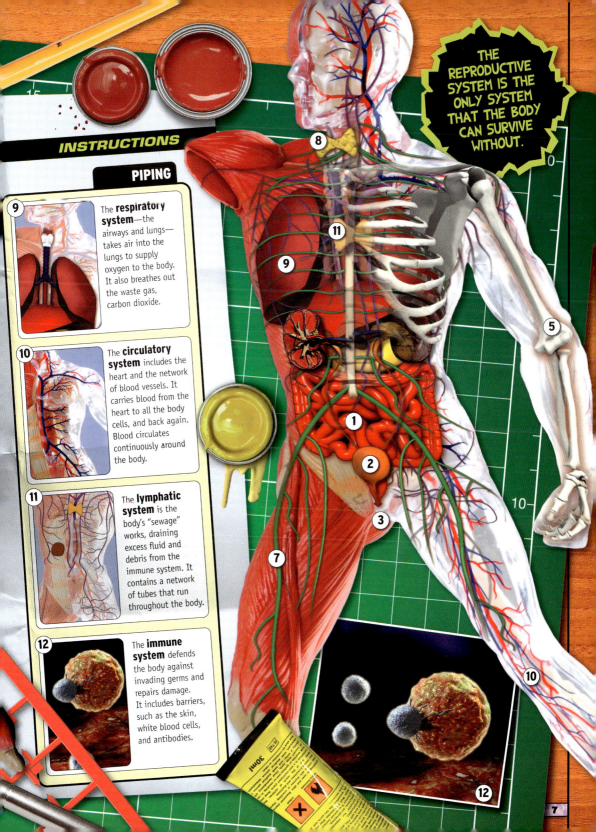

THE REPRODUCTIVE SYSTEM IS THE ONLY SYSTEM THAT THE BODY CAN SURVIVE WITHOUT.

INSTRUCTIONS

PIPING

The **respiratory system**—the airways and lungs—takes air into the lungs to supply oxygen to the body. It also breathes out the waste gas, carbon dioxide.

The **circulatory system** includes the heart and the network of blood vessels. It carries blood from the heart to all the body cells, and back again. Blood circulates continuously around the body.

The **lymphatic system** is the body's "sewage" works, draining excess fluid and debris from the immune system. It contains a network of tubes that run throughout the body.

The **immune system** defends the body against invading germs and repairs damage. It includes barriers, such as the skin, white blood cells, and antibodies.

WILD Landscape

Powerful microscopes have revealed the surface of the body to be surprisingly varied. Close-up, skin looks like rough terrain and hair grows on it like a forest. The skin is such an important organ that it receives more than one third of the body's blood supply.

Hair-raising

Humans are one of the few land mammals to have almost bare skin, so we wear clothes to keep warm. This bare skin, however, helps to keep the body cool. The 100,000 hairs on our heads grow faster than anything else on the body—and under a microscope they look like bumpy tree trunks.

▼ Although just 2 mm thick, the skin is made of various layers.

Mighty overcoat

The skin is the biggest organ in the body and has many important functions. It's waterproof and germproof, insulates the body from the cold and lets out excess heat, responds to touch, and gives the body nourishment by soaking up vitamin D from sunlight.

Scalp hairs grow 2–3 mm each week. Each hair grows for three to five years before it falls out, and a new hair starts to grow.

Shedding skin

To stay effective, skin has to be continually renewed. New cells push up from the dermis to provide the outer layer of protective dead cells in the epidermis. The body loses 40,000 of these dead cells every minute. In a human's lifetime, nearly 100 lb (50 kg) of skin is lost.

ROLLED OUT FLAT, YOUR SKIN WOULD COVER 21 SQ FT (2 SQ M). IT WEIGHS 9 LB (4 KG).

8

Nailing it

Just like hair, nails are made from a tough material called keratin, created when certain cells die and harden. Fingernails grow about 1.5 in (2.5 cm) a year—so, uncut, they could grow 10 ft (3 m) or more in a lifetime. The middle fingernail grows fastest and the thumbnail grows slowest.

▼ The nail plate—the visible part of the nail—is made of a hard, transparent type of keratin.

The outer layer of the skin, or **epidermis**, is a tough coating of overlapping layers of dead skin cells.

Underneath, in the **dermis**, there's a thicker layer containing glands, nerve endings, and touch sensors.

Under that, there's a blanket of fat, called "**subcutaneous fat**," to keep the body warm.

The dermis and fat layers are well supplied with **blood**.

▲ As old skin cells die, they leave a hard protein called keratin on the outside of the skin. Keratin gives the skin a tough, protective outer coat, which eventually flakes off.

GROWING SKIN

Artificial skin can be grown in laboratories. It is used to treat people who have suffered severe burns or skin diseases, as well as for testing the effects of drugs and cosmetics.

▶ Each piece of artificial skin is usually grown from a tiny piece of human skin.

9

CELLULAR Cosmos

The body is made up of 100 trillion microscopic parcels called cells. They come in many shapes and sizes as soft cases of chemicals, each with its own personal set of life instructions in the form of DNA.

SCIENTISTS ESTIMATE THAT ONLY FIVE PERCENT OF THE BODY'S CELLS BELONG TO THE BODY—THE REST ARE BACTERIA.

SOME TYPES OF CELL AUTOMATICALLY DIE WHEN THEY BECOME DAMAGED.

THE CELL ZOO

There are more than 200 different kinds of body cell, such as fat cells and skin cells, each with its own special task. The smallest cells are granules in the brain, and the longest are nerve cells that run through the spinal cord from the brain to the toes.

BLOOD CELLS carry oxygen around the body.

MUSCLE CELLS contract to enable the body to move.

NERVE CELLS carry messages between the brain and the body.

BONE CELLS make bone harden as it forms.

SPERM CELLS carry the male's genes to the egg.

OVUM CELLS contain the female genes, ready for fertilization.

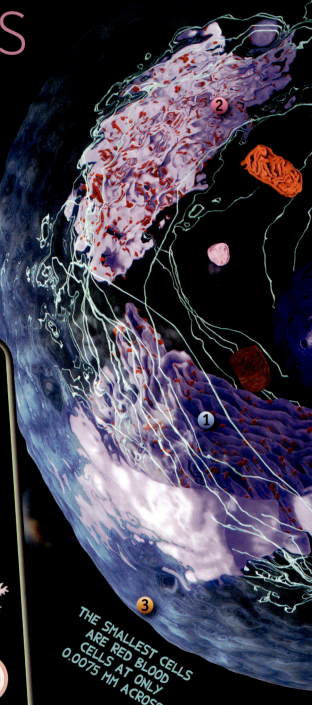

THE SMALLEST CELLS ARE RED BLOOD CELLS AT ONLY 0.0075 MM ACROSS.

Working hard

Every cell is a bustling chemical factory, working every second of the day. Inside each cell, a team of "organelles" perform different tasks. Some transport chemicals to and fro, some break up chemicals, and some make new chemicals, use them, and send them off to other cells. The overall instructions come from the nucleus, but every organelle knows its task.

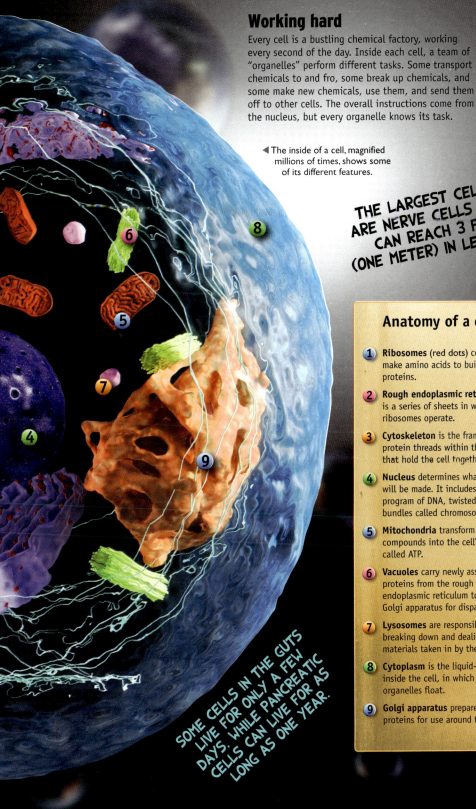

◀ The inside of a cell, magnified millions of times, shows some of its different features.

THE LARGEST CELLS ARE NERVE CELLS AND CAN REACH 3 FT (ONE METER) IN LENGTH.

SOME CELLS IN THE GUTS LIVE FOR ONLY A FEW DAYS, WHILE PANCREATIC CELLS CAN LIVE FOR AS LONG AS ONE YEAR.

Anatomy of a cell

1. **Ribosomes** (red dots) continually make amino acids to build new proteins.

2. **Rough endoplasmic reticulum** is a series of sheets in which ribosomes operate.

3. **Cytoskeleton** is the framework of protein threads within the cell wall that hold the cell together.

4. **Nucleus** determines what proteins will be made. It includes the basic program of DNA, twisted into bundles called chromosomes.

5. **Mitochondria** transform chemical compounds into the cell's fuel, called ATP.

6. **Vacuoles** carry newly assembled proteins from the rough endoplasmic reticulum to the Golgi apparatus for dispatch.

7. **Lysosomes** are responsible for breaking down and dealing with materials taken in by the cell.

8. **Cytoplasm** is the liquid-filled space inside the cell, in which the organelles float.

9. **Golgi apparatus** prepares new proteins for use around the body.

CHEMICAL Plant

The body is made from a mixture of water and organic chemicals, and contains more than half the known chemical elements in the Universe. Every part of the body is involved in changing one chemical to another.

You're wet
The body is more than 60 percent water, found both in cells and body fluids such as blood and lymph. Without water for chemicals to dissolve in, vital reactions could not take place.

You're fat
Much of the body is simply fat. "Essential fat" is needed for particular body tasks—making up 3–5 percent of men's bodies and 8–12 percent of women's. "Storage fat" is fat built up as adipose tissue to give the body an energy reserve. Pads of fat also help to keep out the cold and act as shock absorbers.

▲ Adipose cells are packed with lipids (fat), which store emergency energy reserves.

You're strong
Chemicals called proteins make up about 20 percent of the body. Some proteins are building materials—every cell and tissue is part-protein, including muscles, bones, tendons, hair, nails, and skin. Other proteins make chemical reactions happen (enzymes), send chemical messages (hormones), fight infection (antibodies), or carry oxygen in the blood (hemoglobin).

▶ Blue and red fluorescent dyes show up the protein in throat tissue.

You're sweet

Carbohydrates provide fuel, either circulating in the blood ready for action as simple sugars, or stored as glycogen in the liver and the muscles.

◀ The uterine gland in a pregnant woman's womb secretes glycogen to give the egg energy to grow.

You're made to plan

Nucleic acids are the body's programmers. Deoxyribonucleic acid (DNA) in every cell, passed on from your parents, stores the instructions that tell the body not only how to grow, but also what to do throughout life.

▶ A sample of DNA that has been extracted from body cells.

You're a mineral mine

Bones are partly made of the minerals calcium and phosphorus. Calcium and sodium in the blood, and phosphorus, potassium, and magnesium in the cells, are essential for chemical processes. Iron is crucial to hemoglobin, which carries oxygen in the blood. Traces of other minerals are also vital, including cobalt, copper, iodine, manganese, and zinc.

▶ The calcium in cheese (magnified here) strengthens bones.

You're a gas

The body contains gases, such as oxygen, carbon dioxide, nitrogen oxide, hydrogen, carbon monoxide, and methanethiol. Some are dissolved in fluids and others are bubbles of gas in the lungs or gut.

BODY CHEMICALS

About 99 percent of the mass of the human body is made up of just six elements:

CHEMICAL	%	FOUND
Oxygen	65%	Liquids and tissues, bones, proteins
Carbon	18%	Everywhere
Hydrogen	10%	Liquids and tissues, bones, proteins
Nitrogen	3%	Liquids and tissues, bones, proteins
Calcium	1.5%	Bones, lungs, kidney, liver, thyroid, brain, muscles, heart
Phosphorus	1%	Bones, urine

VITAL Juice

Blood is the body's multitasking transport system. It not only delivers oxygen from the lungs to every body cell, it also carries food to fuel and maintain the cells, and washes away waste to the liver, kidneys, and lungs for disposal. Blood rushes immune cells into action to guard against infection, and even helps to spread body heat.

▼ Scabs are the body's way of protecting a wound from infection.

Plugging a leak

When you cut yourself and bleed from the damaged blood vessels, platelets instantly gather. As they do, they send out an alarm in the form of "clotting factors." These draw in other platelets and encourage them to clump together to make fibers or "fibrin" that plug the leak. The fibrin dries out to form a scab, protecting the wound until it has healed.

COMPLEX MIXTURE

Blood looks red in color, but it is mostly made up of a clear, yellowish fluid called plasma. The color red comes from the red blood cells that are swept along by it. Plasma also contains giant white cells called leucocytes and little lumps called platelets.

▲ Blood cells and fibrin (yellow) rush to a wound to form a clot. This is called coagulation.

THERE'S ABOUT ONE GALLON (4 L) OF BLOOD IN THE BODY.

JUST ONE MOLECULE OF FIBRIN NEEDS TO FORM AT A CUT FOR A CHAIN REACTION OF COAGULATION TO BEGIN—CREATING 30,000 MORE MOLECULES OF FIBRIN ALMOST INSTANTLY.

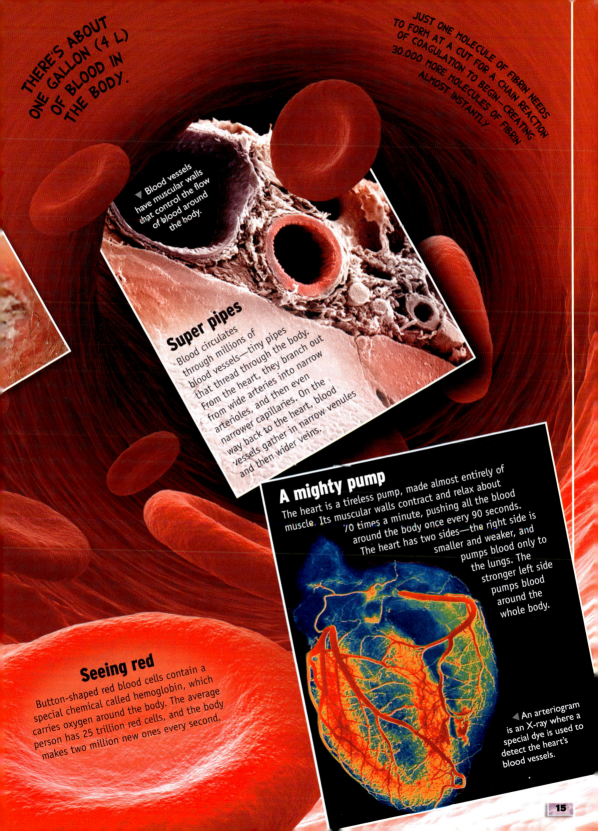

◄ Blood vessels have muscular walls that control the flow of blood around the body.

Super pipes
Blood circulates through millions of blood vessels—tiny pipes that thread through the body. From the heart, they branch out from wide arteries into narrow arterioles, and then even narrower capillaries. On the way back to the heart, blood vessels gather in narrow venules and then wider veins.

A mighty pump
The heart is a tireless pump, made almost entirely of muscle. Its muscular walls contract and relax about 70 times a minute, pushing all the blood around the body once every 90 seconds. The heart has two sides—the right side is smaller and weaker, and pumps blood only to the lungs. The stronger left side pumps blood around the whole body.

Seeing red
Button-shaped red blood cells contain a special chemical called hemoglobin, which carries oxygen around the body. The average person has 25 trillion red cells, and the body makes two million new ones every second.

◄ An arteriogram is an X-ray where a special dye is used to detect the heart's blood vessels.

15

Body Heat

The body cannot survive for long without the continuous input of energy from food. Energy drives all the body's chemical reactions, which release heat energy for warmth and muscle energy for movement.

▼ Some cells only contain one mitochondrion, but others contain thousands.

◄ A thermogram detects heat. Red shows the hottest parts and blue the coldest. The head and chest are the warmest parts of the body.

A trillion fires

Tiny bursts of energy are constantly released inside each of the trillions of body cells in a process called cellular respiration. In each cell, microscopic "furnaces" called mitochondria use oxygen to break down glucose molecules and release energy. This process generates heat.

STORED ENERGY IS PACKED INTO MILLIONS OF TINY MOLECULES CALLED ATP (ADENOSINE TRIPHOSPHATE). ATP IS LIKE A COILED SPRING, READY TO UNWIND AND RELEASE ITS ENERGY.

Hot bodies

For body processes to function well, the body must remain at the perfect temperature—98.6°F (37°C). This is warmer than the outside world, so the body continually generates heat by moving the muscles and triggering chemical reactions in the liver.

ENERGY FOOD
Energy comes from carbohydrates in food, including sugar and starch. Fats in food provide energy, too, but this is stored rather than used immediately. Energy-rich molecules are either delivered to every body cell as glucose in the blood, or temporarily held in the liver as glycogen.

▼ When people play sports, the body sweats to release heat energy.

Stay cool
If the body becomes too hot, the hypothalamus (the brain's "thermostat") tells the body to lose heat by sweating through the skin's pores. Sweating not only takes warm water out of the body, but also cools the skin as the moisture evaporates. The hypothalamus also boosts the supply of blood to the skin to take heat away from the body's core.

Brrrrrrrr...
If the body becomes too cold, the hypothalamus generates heat by boosting cell activity and making the muscles move rapidly in shivers. It also cuts heat loss by restricting the supply of blood to the skin to keep warmth in the body's core.

▲ In 2005, Lewis Gordon Pugh broke the world record for the farthest-north, long-distance swim, by swimming one kilometer through water in cracks between the North Pole ice.

DURING A MATCH, A TOP TENNIS PLAYER USES ENOUGH ENERGY TO BOIL A KETTLE EVERY MINUTE.

ROUGH SKIN
When the body is cold, hairs on the skin may stand on end, creating "goose bumps." This traps a layer of warm air next to the skin, making the body feel warmer.

Human COMPUTER

The brain contains more than 100 billion nerve cells, or neurons. Each neuron is connected to as many as 25,000 other neurons—creating trillions of routes for signals to buzz around the body. This enables us to think and learn, jump and sit, and laugh and cry—everything that makes us human.

RECEIVING SIGNALS
The cerebral cortex is the wrinkled layer of interconnected nerve cells around the outside of the brain. It is made up of different structures, each with individual functions. Many sense signals are received and responded to here.

The demanding brain
The brain makes up less than two percent of the body's weight, yet demands more than 20 percent of its blood supply. Deprived of the oxygen blood carries for even a few moments, brain cells quickly die. If the blood supply is cut off entirely, the brain loses consciousness in ten seconds and death occurs within a few minutes.

◀ Blood floods into the brain continuously through large arteries to give it energy for thinking.

PREFRONTAL CORTEX is involved with memory, solving problems, and judgment.

A brain of two halves
The brain is split into two halves or hemispheres, linked by a bundle of nerves. The left half controls the right side of the body and the right half controls the left side of the body. It is believed that the left side deals with logical and analytical thinking, while the right side expresses emotion and creativity.

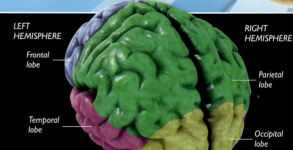

LEFT HEMISPHERE
Frontal lobe
Temporal lobe

RIGHT HEMISPHERE
Parietal lobe
Occipital lobe

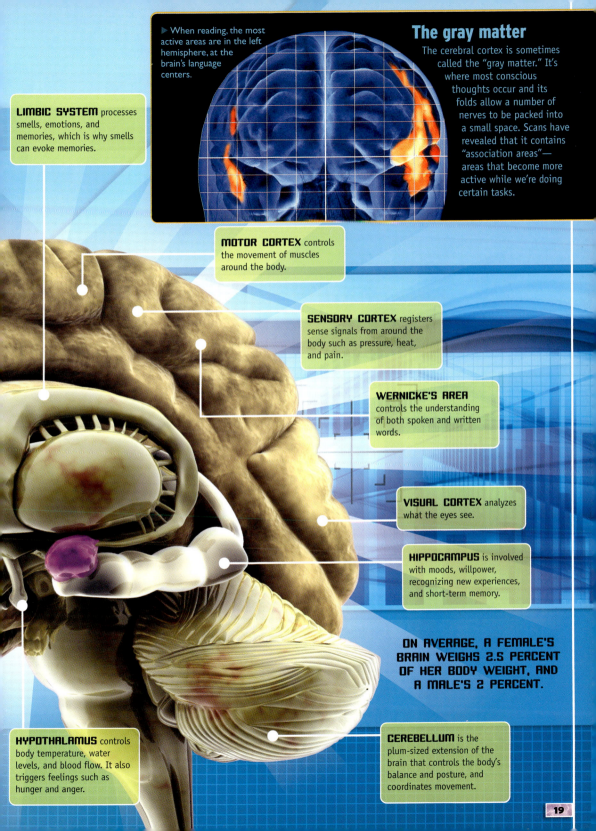

▶ When reading, the most active areas are in the left hemisphere, at the brain's language centers.

The gray matter
The cerebral cortex is sometimes called the "gray matter." It's where most conscious thoughts occur and its folds allow a number of nerves to be packed into a small space. Scans have revealed that it contains "association areas"— areas that become more active while we're doing certain tasks.

LIMBIC SYSTEM processes smells, emotions, and memories, which is why smells can evoke memories.

MOTOR CORTEX controls the movement of muscles around the body.

SENSORY CORTEX registers sense signals from around the body such as pressure, heat, and pain.

WERNICKE'S AREA controls the understanding of both spoken and written words.

VISUAL CORTEX analyzes what the eyes see.

HIPPOCAMPUS is involved with moods, willpower, recognizing new experiences, and short-term memory.

ON AVERAGE, A FEMALE'S BRAIN WEIGHS 2.5 PERCENT OF HER BODY WEIGHT, AND A MALE'S 2 PERCENT.

HYPOTHALAMUS controls body temperature, water levels, and blood flow. It also triggers feelings such as hunger and anger.

CEREBELLUM is the plum-sized extension of the brain that controls the body's balance and posture, and coordinates movement.

Body SIGNALING

Nerves make up the body's communication network. They carry instant messages from the brain to every part of the body—and stream back a constant flow of data to tell the brain what's going on both inside the body and in the outside world.

Bundle of nerves

The brain stem, spinal cord, and branches of the peripheral nervous system are made of long bundles of nerve fibers called nerves. These bundles are made from the axons (tails) of nerve cells, bound together like the wires in a telephone cable. Signals can travel at up to 395 ft (120 m) per second.

▶ Nerve fibers are bundled together and insulated by a sheath of fatty myelin to keep the signal strong.

Body network

The central nervous system is made up of the brain and the spinal cord—the nerves in the spine. It is responsible for collecting information fed in through nerves from all over the body, processing data, and sending out responses. The nerves of the peripheral nervous system branch out from the central nervous system to every limb and body part.

SCIENTISTS LEARNED HOW HUMAN NERVES WORK BY STUDYING THE NERVES OF SQUID.

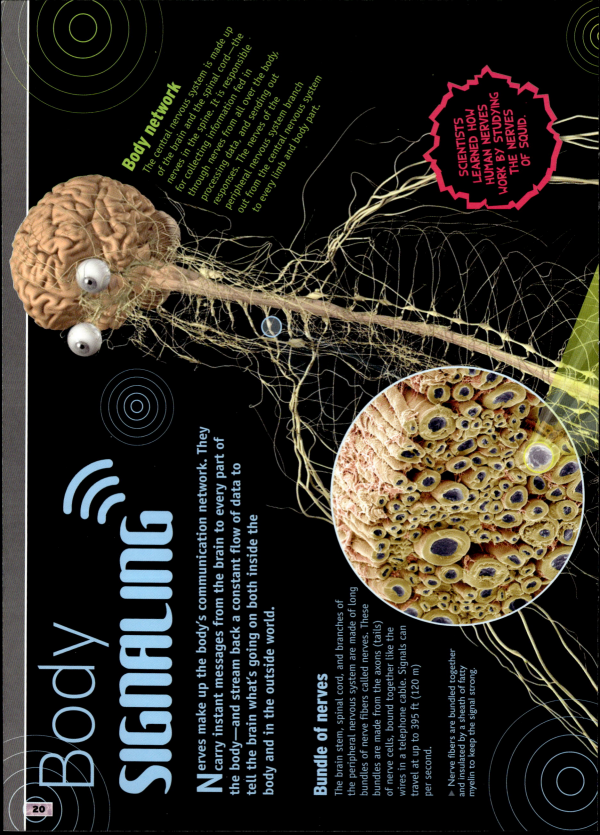

Living connector

A nerve cell, or neuron, is shaped like a spider, with a nucleus at the center, lots of branching threads called dendrites, and a winding tail called an axon. From each neuron, electrical signals buzz through the dendrites, along the axon, and out to other neurons.

▶ Nerve signals are transmitted as waves of electrically charged potassium and sodium particles.

AUTOPILOT

Reflexes are muscle movements that happen without conscious thought. Humans are born with some of these automatic movements, such as urinating. Others are learned, such as drinking from a glass without thinking about it.

TOUCH ME

You might think you have just five senses—sight, hearing, smell, taste, and touch. However, the skin is covered with at least five kinds of sense receptor. There are different receptors for pain, heat, cold, touch, and pressure. Some receptors, called Pacinian receptors, respond quickly and then stop, while others, called Ruffini receptors, respond slowly but then keep going.

Mind the gap

Neurons don't touch each other. Instead, they transmit signals across a tiny gap or "synapse," as streams of chemical particles called neurotransmitters. As the droplets of neurotransmitter signal arrives. Droplets whenever a nerve signal arrives. synapse of neurotransmitter lock onto the receiving nerve's receptors, they fire the signal onward.

▶ There are thought to be 100–500 trillion synapses in the brain.

21

EYE OPENER

YOUR AWESOME EYES COMBINE THE PICTURE QUALITY OF THE BEST DIGITAL CAMERAS WITH A VERSATILITY THAT NO CAMERA CAN MATCH. THEY CAN FOCUS BOTH ON A SPECK OF DUST INCHES AWAY AND A GALAXY FAR ACROSS THE UNIVERSE, AND WORK IN BOTH STARLIGHT AND SUNLIGHT.

Black hole
The dark "pupil" is a porthole that lets light into the eye. It looks black because the eye is so dark inside. When light gets very dim, the fringe or "iris" around it can open wide to let more light in.

▼ The pattern of fibers in the iris is unique to each human, so it can be used to identify individuals, just like fingerprints.

▼ A damaged cornea can cause blurred vision. To restore normal eyesight, surgeons lift the top layer of the cornea and trim it minutely with a laser.

Stay sharp
The cornea is the transparent window at the front of the eye that gives the main focusing power. Light rays pass through the cornea and are refracted (bent) before hitting the lens. The lens adjusts the focus to give a sharp picture, whether you are looking at something close-up or far away. Each adjustment takes barely one fiftieth of a second.

Movie time
The inside of the eyeball is like a mini cinema. The cornea and lens project an image onto the back of the eye, called the retina. Although the image is just a few millimeters across inside the eye, you see it at its real size.

THE EYES CONSTANTLY SCAN THE SCENE YOU ARE LOOKING AT IN INCREDIBLY RAPID MOVEMENTS TO BUILD UP A PICTURE AND PICK OUT KEY DETAILS.

▲ When the muscles surrounding the lens contract, the lens becomes thicker and can focus on close-up objects.

▼ There are only seven colors in the rainbow, but the eye's cones can distinguish ten million colors!

Taking the picture
The retina acts like the photocells in a camera—150 million rods detect if it's dark or light, and even work in very low light, while eight million cones detect colors and work best in daylight.

Highway to the brain
It's actually the brain that "sees," not the eyes, using the visual cortex. When light hits the retina, the rods and cones send nerve signals down the optic nerve to create a picture in the brain.

▼ Signals from the right side of each retina go to the right of the visual cortex; those from the left of each retina go to the left of the visual cortex.

NEW Life

The human body can create a new version of itself. It starts when two single, microscopically tiny cells—a male's sperm cell and a female's egg cell—join. From this combined cell a new life begins, as a baby slowly grows inside the female's womb for the nine months of pregnancy.

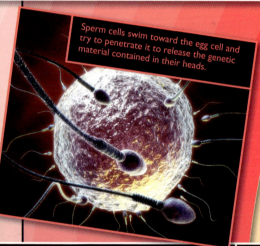

Sperm cells swim toward the egg cell and try to penetrate it to release the genetic material contained in their heads.

AFTER ONLY ONE WEEK, THE EMBRYO CONTAINS HUNDREDS OF CELLS.

Fertilized egg to embryo

As soon as the sperm and egg join successfully, the egg is fertilized, and the new life is "conceived." The egg immediately begins to divide rapidly, making seemingly identical copies of itself to create an embryo. As the cells multiply, differences appear, and layers that will become skin and organs develop.

Day 1
Millions try, but in most cases, only one sperm cell will succeed and fertilize the egg cell.

Day 6
The ball of cells attaches to the lining of the female's womb.

Day 40

In the beginning

The sperm and egg are special not because they have something extra, but because they have something missing. Unlike other body cells, they have only one set of 23 chromosomes, not the usual two. The sperm must add its 23 chromosomes to the egg's 23 chromosomes to make the full complement of 46 and start a new life. This happens during sexual intercourse, when the male's sperm swim into the female's womb to reach the egg.

IF TWO EGGS ARE RELEASED AT THE SAME TIME AND ARE BOTH FERTILIZED, NON-IDENTICAL TWINS DEVELOP.

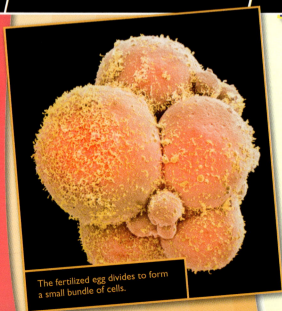

The fertilized egg divides to form a small bundle of cells.

Embryo to fetus

After about 40 days, the embryo, though barely as big as a pea, has developed some recognizable features, such as a nose, mouth, and ears. Dark spots show where the eyes will grow. A heart beats rapidly inside, and a brain, muscles, and bones start to grow. After nine weeks, the embryo has become so babylike (though with a giant head) that it is described as a fetus, not an embryo.

At this early stage, the embryo looks like a tadpole.

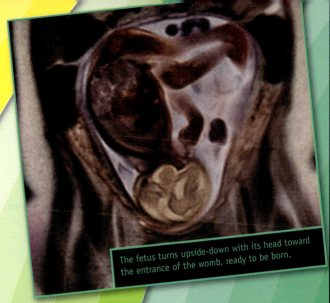

The fetus turns upside-down with its head toward the entrance of the womb, ready to be born.

Growing strong

At the halfway stage, the fetus looks like a curled-up baby, only smaller and less defined. It's only about the size of an adult's hand, so still has some way to grow, but it begins to move around and may even kick its developing legs inside the mother's womb. Research suggests the baby may even be able to hear things outside its mother's body.

Time for birth

Finally, after about 37 weeks, the fetus is fully developed. Birth begins when the mother goes into "labor." Firstly, the womb muscles contract and burst the bag of fluid that surrounds the baby. Secondly, the muscles around the womb's neck contract and relax rhythmically to push the baby out through the birth canal.

The embryo is now about 5 mm long and buds for the arms and legs start to develop.

Day 133
The fetus is now about 6.5 in (16 cm) long and fine, downy hair covers its body.

Day 266
The fetus is about 14 in (36 cm) long and has a firm grip.

An ultrasound scanner reveals the baby growing inside the womb.

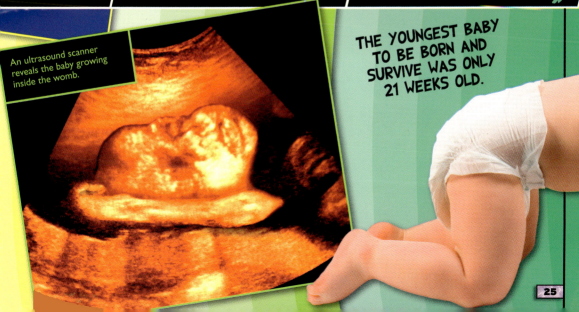

THE YOUNGEST BABY TO BE BORN AND SURVIVE WAS ONLY 21 WEEKS OLD.

GROWTH Factor

The rate at which the body grows depends on age and gender—babies and teenagers grow rapidly, and males become taller than females. Body proportions also develop with age—a baby's legs only make up one quarter of its length, but by adulthood the legs equal half of the body's height.

Big head
A newborn baby's head is already three-quarters of its adult size because it contains the brain. There are two gaps called fontanelles between the bones of a baby's skull, where there is only membrane (a "skin" of thin tissue), not bone. This allows the skull to flex, so there is room for the brain to grow even more. The gaps close and the bones join together after about 18 months.

BABIES HAVE A MUCH STRONGER SENSE OF SMELL THAN ADULTS.

Time to grow
Children grow quickly because the brain is continually sending out a "grow-faster" chemical. This growth hormone is secreted by the pituitary gland in the center of the brain. It tells cells to make protein and break down fat for energy. Too much growth hormone can cause a condition called gigantism, or acromegaly where the body grows too big and in the wrong places.

6 months–1 year
A baby begins to grow teeth—the upper and lower incisors come first.

1–4 years
Toddlers start to talk from one year old and can read simple words from four years old.

9–13 years

◂ For the first nine months or more, babies can only move on their hands and knees.

◂ Toddlers only gradually develop the strength and balance to walk upright.

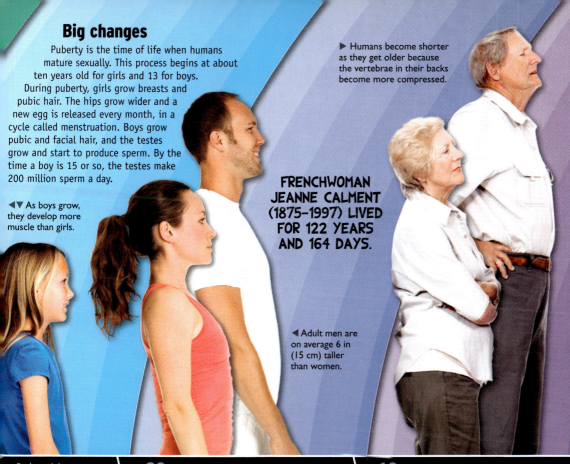

Big changes

Puberty is the time of life when humans mature sexually. This process begins at about ten years old for girls and 13 for boys. During puberty, girls grow breasts and pubic hair. The hips grow wider and a new egg is released every month, in a cycle called menstruation. Boys grow pubic and facial hair, and the testes grow and start to produce sperm. By the time a boy is 15 or so, the testes make 200 million sperm a day.

◄▼ As boys grow, they develop more muscle than girls.

► Humans become shorter as they get older because the vertebrae in their backs become more compressed.

FRENCHWOMAN JEANNE CALMENT (1875–1997) LIVED FOR 122 YEARS AND 164 DAYS.

◄ Adult men are on average 6 in (15 cm) taller than women.

During adolescence a boy grows about 3.75 in (9.5 cm) a year and a girl 3.35 in (8.5 cm).

20+ years
Early adulthood is from 20 to 39 years and "middle age" is from 40 to 59 years.

60+ years
In old age, eyesight and hearing often weaken.

All grownup
By the age of 20, the body is fully developed and at its physical peak. By the early 30s, the body begins to lose strength, speed, and agility. Between the ages of 45–55, most women go through the menopause and become unable to get pregnant naturally.

Old age
As the body grows older, it stops renewing itself so well—the muscles weaken, bones become more brittle, joints stiffen, and the skin starts to slacken and wrinkle. The hair may eventually turn gray as pigment cells stop working.

MUSCLE Power

IF ALL THE MUSCLES IN THE BODY PULLED TOGETHER, THEY COULD LIFT A BUS.

Every move the body makes needs muscles, from lifting a finger to jumping in the air—even for sitting still. Without muscles, the body would slump like a sack of potatoes. Muscles are amazing little motors that work instantly, whenever they are needed, by constantly contracting and relaxing.

Running on air

Ideally, muscles work aerobically—the cells get enough oxygen from glucose to release energy. However, if a person is unfit or has worked the muscles too hard, the cells may burn glucose "anaerobically"—without oxygen. This uses up glucose rapidly, making the body tired and leaving a buildup of lactic acid, which makes the muscles sore. To draw in the extra oxygen needed to burn this lactic acid, you pant when you stop running.

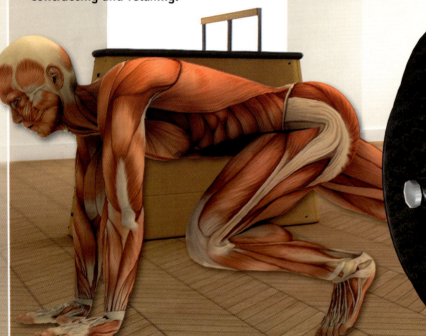

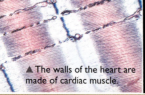

▲ The walls of the heart are made of cardiac muscle.

Outside and in

The body has two kinds of muscle—voluntary muscles that are under conscious control and involuntary muscles that work automatically. Voluntary muscles cover the skeleton and allow the body to move. Involuntary muscles control bodily functions, such as the heartbeat.

Power stripes

Muscles get their power from bundles of fibers that contract and relax. Inside each fiber are alternating, interlocking stripes or "filaments" of actin and myosin. When the brain tells a muscle to contract, little buds on each myosin filament twist, pulling on the actin filaments and making the muscle shorter. Each time a muscle contracts, another muscle fiber needs to shorten in the opposite direction to pull it back to its original length.

▶ Muscles work in pairs of actin and myosin filaments because they can only shorten themselves.

THE STRONGEST MUSCLES ARE THE MASSETER MUSCLES, WHICH CONTROL THE JAW'S BITING MOVEMENT.

▲ The body has several layers of muscle. Most are attached to bones with tough fibers called tendons.

Muscle building

During exercise, the muscles grow larger. At first, the fibers simply grow fatter. With regular exercise, the body grows new muscle fibers, which means they become stronger. The blood supply improves, too, so the muscles can work longer without tiring.

▶ Fibers in the voluntary muscles move the bones.

On demand

There are 640 voluntary muscles on the skeleton. The brain can only consciously control combinations that work together, rather than individual muscles. The longest is the sartorius muscle at the front of the thigh, while the biggest is the gluteus maximus in the buttocks.

STRONG Structure

Bones give the body a strong, rigid, light framework. Bone can stand being squeezed twice as much as granite and stretched four times as much as concrete. Yet it's so light that bone accounts for barely 14 percent of the body's weight.

A lasting framework
The skeleton is made of 206 bones. As living tissue, the bones are constantly replenished with new cells that grow in the bone's center, called the marrow. The skeleton is the only body part that survives long after death.

THE HAND AND WRIST HAVE ABOUT 30 SMALL JOINTS.

Living bones
Bones are packed with living cells called osteocytes. Each osteocyte sits in a little pocket called a lacuna, and is constantly washed in blood. Some, called osteoblasts, make new bone. Others, called osteoclasts, break down the old, worn-out bone. The soft spongy center or "marrow" of bone produces new blood cells.

The tiniest bone is in **the ear**. It's called the stirrup bone and is only 3 mm long.

▲ Inside osteoblast cells, lumps of calcium salts crystallize to make hard bone.

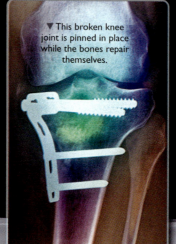

▼ This broken knee joint is pinned in place while the bones repair themselves.

Broken bones
Bones are strong, but they can break or "fracture." Most fractures heal—the body stems any bleeding, then gradually fills the gap with osteoblasts, which weave new bone across the break. The break may need to be straightened and the bone held in place with pins or a plaster cast to ensure it repairs in the right way.

The **appendicular skeleton** is the 126 bones that hang off the axial skeleton—the shoulders, arms and hands, and hips, legs, and feet.

The **axial skeleton** is the 80 bones of the upper body, including the skull, spine, ribs, and breastbone.

Bone strength

Bones are an engineering triumph. Being hollow makes them light. Their strength comes from a combination of flexible collagen fibers and honeycomb struts called trabeculae. Trabeculae are thin but perfectly angled to resist stresses.

◀ The network of trabeculae inside a bone make it both strong and light.

▼ The human foot has 26 bones and 33 joints for balance and mobility.

WITH EVERY STEP, THE THIGH BONE BEARS A CRUNCHING PRESSURE OF 450 LB PER SQ IN (31 KG PER SQ CM).

Mobile skeleton

The skeleton is strong and rigid, yet can bend. It's made of lots of separate bones that are linked by flexible joints. At the joints, bones are held together by fibers called ligaments and cushioned by smooth, rubbery cartilage.

31

ALIEN INVADERS

You might think you're clean, but you're actually a zoo of microscopic bugs. Living inside your guts are up to 1,000 different species of bacteria—and a similar number are encamped on your skin. Then there are fungi and viruses, mosquitoes, fleas, bedbugs, blackflies, botflies, lice, leeches, ticks, mites, and worms...

Very lice

The head louse (*plural* lice) is a tiny insect that has made human hair its only home for thousands of years. Lice are just big enough to see with the naked eye. They cannot fly, and spend all their lives crawling through their host's hair sucking tiny amounts of blood from the scalp.

Mite have

Your feet, wrists, genitals, and the roots of your hairs are home to a little bug—the follicle mite. Mites are related to spiders, but they are so small, even as adults (less than 0.25 mm long), that you can't see them with the naked eye.

◀ These tiny mites live in the roots of human eyelashes.

◀ The head louse spends its entire life in human hair.

RESISTANCE IS FUTILE!

IN 1991, DOCTORS REMOVED A 37-FT- (11-M-) LONG TAPEWORM FROM AMERICAN SALLY MAE WALLACE'S GUT.

Got you taped
In some parts of the world, people who have eaten uncooked meat end up with flat, ribbonlike tapeworms living in their gut. These worms settle in and feed off the food the infected person eats, soon making their host ill. They are so flat and the human guts are so long that they can grow to more than 30 ft (9 m) in length!

▲ The head of a tapeworm has suckers for gripping the inside of the gut.

Coli wobbles
About 0.1 percent of the bacteria living in the gut belongs to the strain *Escherichia coli*. Most *E coli* are harmless, but occasionally they can make you ill with food poisoning. They enter the body on unwashed vegetables or in uncooked meat, then multiply and release floods of toxins in the intestines.

▼ Under UV light, bacteria can be seen on the hands.

▲ *E coli* bacteria live in your gut and supply you with vitamins K2 and B1.

Skin bugs
A powerful microscope reveals your skin is absolutely crawling with tiny bacteria. Many are Actinobacteria, which are also common in soil. Although there are many billions of bacteria living on your skin, they are so small, their combined volume is no bigger than a pea.

MILLIONS ARE COMING!

Repair and Rebuild

The body is remarkably good at shielding itself against harm and repairing any damage. Sometimes, though, it needs medical help. Vaccines arm the body's immune system against future infections, antibiotic drugs kill many disease-causing bacteria, and surgery corrects defects.

▶ This titanium knee joint (red) replaced a knee destroyed by bone disease.

New joints

Bones are tough, but can be damaged, especially at the joints. With the aid of special materials such as titanium, surgeons can remove a damaged joint and replace it with an artificial one that lasts for ten years. By using a computer to visualize the replacement, it is always a perfect match.

Bionic bodies

Artificial hands and limbs respond to nerve signals directly from the brain. Therefore a person only has to think to control the tiny electric motors that make a bionic, or prosthetic, hand move. Bionics are used to replace lost or irreversibly damaged hands or limbs. In the future, soldiers may have extra bionics to give them "super powers."

▼ Scottish firefighter Ian Reid, who lost his hand in an accident, has a bionic replacement that can grip as tightly as a real hand.

ADD-ON POWERED LIMBS COULD ENABLE A SOLDIER TO RUN UP A HILL CARRYING MORE THAN 650 LB (300 KG).

▶ This replacement bladder was grown on a mold from stem cells in just five weeks.

Organ growing

Scientists can now make replacement body parts in the laboratory. They start with special "stem" cells that can grow into any kind of cell. The stem cells form into the right shape on a special mold of microfibers. Once the new organ has grown, the mold dissolves and the organ can be transplanted into the body.

Disease control

Many deadly diseases have been brought under control using vaccination. This is where the body is infected with a weakened or "dead" version of a germ. In response, the body builds up antibodies, so it is ready to fight back if ever exposed to the real disease.

New cells for old

Stem cells can grow into almost any other kind of cell. In the future, stem cells may be produced to make cells that replace faulty ones. Scientists may then be able to treat anything from cancer to multiple sclerosis, blindness, and even baldness.

◀ Faulty organs might be repaired by using stem cells from embryos such as this three-day-old human embryo.

▲ Smallpox caused about 400 million deaths during the 20th century. It was finally eradicated by vaccination in the 1970s.

IN 2011, A MAN WAS GIVEN A NEW THROAT GROWN FROM STEM CELLS—THE FIRST LAB-GROWN REPLACEMENT ORGAN.

CHEMICAL Messengers

How does the body know when to grow and by how much? How does it cope with stress? How does it keep thousands of substances in the right balance? The complex task of controlling the body is managed by an extraordinary system of chemicals called hormones.

Stop & Go

Hormones work automatically using clever "feedback" systems. The liver supplies the blood with the energy chemical glucose. If glucose levels rise too high, the pancreas releases the hormone insulin, which feeds back to the liver, triggering it to stop supplying glucose.

▲ Islets of Langerhans cells in the pancreas release hormones to control sugar levels in the blood.

▼ Thyroglobulin (shown in orange) makes thyroid hormones to control the body's energy usage.

Hormones and glands

Hormones are chemicals that have particular effects on certain cells. "Endocrine" glands release tiny drops of hormone into the blood to spread around the body. Each gland releases its own type of hormone, and each hormone has a special task.

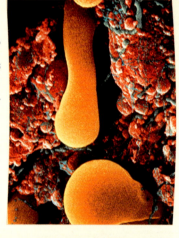

THE PITUITARY GLAND WEIGHS LESS THAN ONE GRAM, BUT IT IS ONE OF THE MOST IMPORTANT ORGANS IN THE BODY.

Grow-faster chemicals

The thyroid gland in the neck and pituitary gland in the brain are no bigger than cherries, but supply vital hormones to make sure the body grows normally. The three thyroid hormones control how fast cells burn energy. The pituitary gland makes the growth hormone, which controls how fast cells grow and multiply.

▼ Too much growth hormone can make the body grow unusually big. Sultan Kösen has the largest handspan in the world at 12 in (30.5 cm) wide.

ARTIFICIALLY MADE STEROID HORMONES CAN BE USED IN INHALERS TO REDUCE THE EFFECTS OF ASTHMA.

Adrenaline rush

A sudden scare prepares the body for danger, as it triggers a flood of the hormones adrenaline and noradrenaline. As the hormones rush into the blood, they make the heartbeat faster and stronger. This boosts the blood supply to the muscles to help you run or fight. The blood supply to the skin is restricted, making it go pale and cold. The eyes widen, giving better vision.

▶ During extreme bungee jumping, the body releases hormones to prepare for "fight or flight."

Time for change

At a certain age, known as puberty, sex hormones start to be released into the body. A female's ovaries make estrogen and progesterone, which control the menstrual cycle. A male's testes make testosterone, which promotes the production of sperm and creates characteristics such as a deep voice and bigger muscles.

▼ When blood is evaporated, the sex hormone testosterone is left behind as crystals.

INDEX

Entries in **bold** refer to main subject entries; entries in *italics* refer to illustrations.

acromegaly 26
actin 29
adipose tissue 12, *12*
adolescence 27
adrenaline 39
adulthood 27
aerobic/anaerobic 28
amino acids 11
antibiotics 36
antibodies 7, 12, 37
appendicular skeleton 31, *31*
arteries 15, 18, *18*
arteriograms 15, *15*
artificial joints and limbs 36, *36*
artificial skin 9, *9*
ATP 11, 16
axial skeleton 31, *31*
axons 20, 21

babies 25, 26, *26*
bacteria 10, 32, 33, *33*, 36
bionic limbs 36, *36*
birth 25
bladder 6, 37, *37*
blood 7, 9, *9*, 13, **14–15**, *14–15*, 18, 30, 39
blood cells 7, 10, *10*, 14, *14*, 15, *15*, 30
blood clots 14, *14*
blood vessels 7, 15, *15*
body systems **6–7**, *6–7*
body temperature 16
bone cells 10, *10*
bone fractures 30, *30*
bone marrow 30
bones 12, 13, 26, 27, **30–1**, *30–1*
brain 6, 10, **18–19**, *18–19*, 21, 23, 26, 29
bugs **32–3**, *32–3*

calcium 13, *13*, 30, *30*
capillaries 15
carbohydrates 13, 17
carbon dioxide 7, 13
cardiac muscle 15, 28, *28*
cartilage 31
cells 6, **10–11**, *10–11*
 adipose cells 12, *12*
 blood cells 7, 10, *10*, 14, *14*, 15, *15*, 30
 bone cells 10, *10*
 division 24, *24*
 egg cells 24, *24*
 muscle cells 10, *10*
 nerve cells 10, *10*, 18, 20, 21
 osteoblast cells 30
 ovum cells 10, *10*
 pancreatic cells 11
 skin cells 8, 9, *9*
 sperm cells 10, *10*, 24, *24*
 stem cells 37
cellular respiration 16
central nervous system 20
cerebellum 19, *19*

cerebral cortex 18, *18–19*, 19
chemicals **12–13**, 26, **38–9**
chromosomes 11, 24
circulatory system 6, 7, *7*, 15
coagulation 14, 15
collagen 31
cones 23
cornea 22, *22*, 23
cytoplasm 11, *11*
cytoskeleton *10*, 11

death 18
dendrites 21
digestive system 6, *6*, *7*
DNA 11, 13, *13*

egg cells 24, *24*
embryos 24, 25, *25*, 37, *37*
endocrine system 6, *6*, *7*, 38
energy 6, 12, **16–17**, 28, 38, 39
enzymes 12
Escheria coli (*E coli*) 33, *33*
estrogen 39
exercise 17, 29, 39
eyes **22–3**, *22–3*, 39

fat 9, *9*, 12, 17
fetus 25, *25*
fibrin 14, *14*, 15
follicle mites 32, *32*
fontanelles 26
food poisoning 33

germs 7
gigantism 26
glands 6, 9, 26
glucose 17, 28, 38
glycogen 13, 17
Golgi apparatus 11, *11*
goose bumps 17
gray matter 19
growth **26–7**, 39

hair 8, *8*, 12, 27, 32
head lice 32, *32*
heart 15, *15*, 28, 39
heat energy 16, 17
hemispheres of the brain 18, *18*, 19
hemoglobin 12, 13, 15
hippocampus 19, *19*
hormones 6, 12, 26, **38–9**
hypothalamus 17, 19, *19*

immune system 7, *7*, 14, 36
insulin 38
integumentary system 6, *6*
iris 22, *22*
iron 13
Islets of Langerhans 38, *38*

joints 27, 30, *30*, 31, 36, *36*

keratin 9
kidneys 6

lactic acid 28
lens 22, 23, *23*

leucocytes 14
ligaments 31
limbic system 19, *19*
lipids 12
liver 13, 16, 17, 38
lungs 7, 15
lymphatic system 7, *7*
lysosomes 11, *11*

memory 18, 19
menopause 27
menstruation 27, 39
mitochondria 11, *11*, 16
motor cortex 19, *19*
muscle cells 10, *10*
muscle fibers 29
muscles 6, *6*, 12, 13, 15, 16, 17, 25, 27, **28–9**, *28*, *29*, 39
 contraction 29
 involuntary 28
 voluntary 28, 29
muscular system 6, *6*
myelin 20
myosin 29

nails 9, *9*, 12
nerve cells 10, *10*, 18, 20, 21
nerve fibers 20, *20*
nerves 6, 19, **20–1**
nervous system 6, *6*, *7*, **20–1**, *20–1*
neurons *see* nerve cells
neurotransmitters 21
noradrenaline 39
nucleic acids 13
nucleus 11, *11*, 21

old age 27
optic nerve 23
organelles 11
organs, replacement 37, *37*
osteoblasts 30
osteocytes 30
ovaries 39
ovum cells 10, *10*
oxygen 7, 12, 13, 15, 16, 18, 28

Pacinian receptors 21
pancreas 38
pancreatic cells 11
peripheral nervous system 20
pituitary gland 26, 38, 39
plasma 14
platelets 14
potassium 13, 21
prefrontal cortex 18, *18*
pregnancy 24–5, 27
progesterone 39
proteins 11, 12, *12*, 26
puberty 27, 39
pupil 22, *22*

reflexes 21
reproductive system 6, *6*, 7, *7*, **24–5**
respiratory system 7, *7*
retina 23
ribosomes *10*, 11

rods 23
rough endoplasmic reticulum *10*, 11
Ruffini receptors 21

scabs 14, *14*
sense receptors 6, 9, 21
sensory cortex 19, *19*
sex hormones 39
sex organs 6
sexual intercourse 24
skeletal system 6, *6*, 7, **30–1**, *30–1*
skin 6, 7, **8–9**, *8–9*, 12, 17, 21, 27, 39
 artificial skin 9, *9*
 cells 8, 9, *9*
 dermis 9, *9*
 epidermis 9, *9*
 shedding 8, 9
 subcutaneous fat 9, *9*
smallpox 37, *37*
sperm 24, 27, 39
sperm cells 10, *10*, 24, *24*
spinal cord 20
stem cells 37
steroids 39
stirrup bone 30, *30*
stomach 6
subcutaneous fat 9, *9*
sweat 17
synapses 21

tapeworms 33, *33*
tendons 12, 29
testosterone 39, *39*
thermograms 16, *16*
thought and feelings 18, 19
thyroglobulin 38, *38*
thyroid gland 39
toddlers 26, *26*
trabeculae 31, *31*
twins 24

urinary system 6, *6*, 7
uterine gland 13, *13*

vaccines 36, 37
vacuoles 11, *11*
veins 15
vertebrae 27
vision 19, **22–3**, 39
visual cortex 19, *19*, 23

water 6, 12
Wernicke's area 19, *19*
womb 13, 24, 25, *25*